Craft Your Calling

Craft Your Calling

A 30-day Warm Up Before Your Training Begins

by

Marc Casciani

eBooks2go

Your Author Journey Begins Here

"Where *What Color is Your Parachute* meets *Purpose Driven Life.*"

- Hollis Haff. Pastor of Discipleship, New Community Church

DEDICATION

For my children, Dallas and Jarah, who are good and perfect gifts in my life. May you live up to the life which God called you.

HOW TO READ THIS BOOK

Read each DAY just after you wake up in the morning and just before you fall asleep at night. Let your mind reflect on the reading for a few minutes. By doing this for 30 days, it will become a good habit.

ACKNOWLEDGMENTS

There are a countless number of people that contributed to the creation of this book but I did want to list a few names to show my undying appreciation.

Deborah Casciani, Carrie Chappie, Thomas Paolo, Ron Graziani, John Goda, Christine Bradley, Penny Cala, David Kovscek, Matthew Turk, Kevin Brighton, David and Virgina Casciani, Mark Milliken, Leslie Humes, David Harlan, Joe Johns, Jonathan McCauley, Todd Casciani, Cynthia Hartnett, Luke Harris, Elaine Lesko, Kevin Muchnok, Thomas Krahe, Brian Dworkin, Patricia Hanna, Lee Parks, Donna Boeggema, James Fawcett, Katarzyna Swope, Dr. Brian Miller, Daniel Abraham, Gina M. Nalitt, John Fedkoe, Trevor Davis, Kent Gordon, Matt Knizner, Martin and Holly Muchnok, Joseph Hughes, Corey and Michelle Weaver, Julius "Bill" Contz, James Anderson, Kevin Cook, Tyler Grimes, Richard Goodman, Eric Gazica, Andrew Chiapusio, Erico Casciani, Michele Johnson, Michele and Jeff Conway, Kim Goodrich, Rich Namath, Matt Fitzgibbons, Dan Mularski, Scott Addis, Tom Onestak, Mary Susan Yurek, John Holt, Jamie Heynes, Mark Bolton, Stacy Richter, Tom Gillooly, Chris Georgulis, Julie Labuszewski, Hollis Haff, John Folino, and Gary Jenkins.

Thank you all and you are appreciated beyond measure.

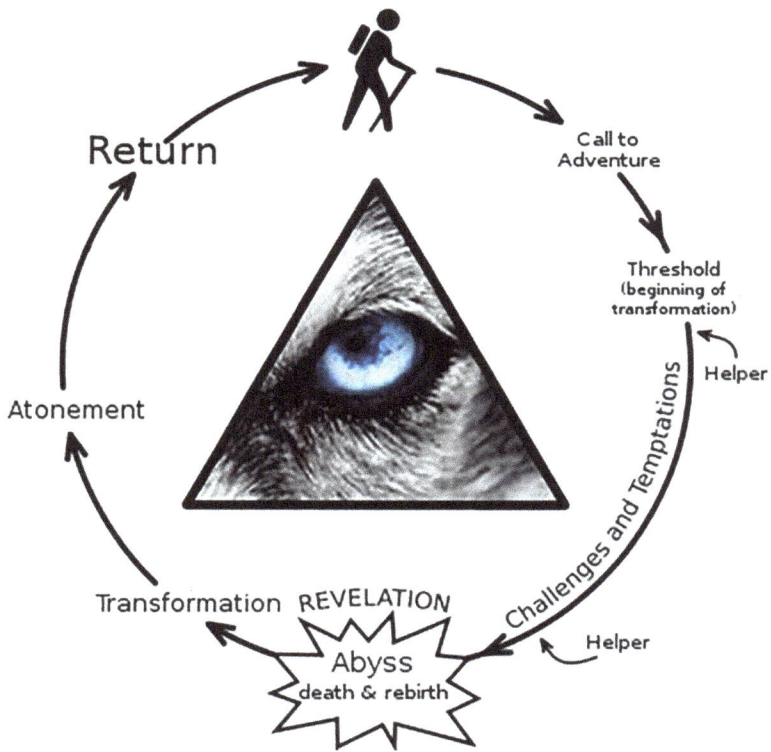

Quantity Purchases:
Companies, professional groups, clubs, and other organizations may qualify for special terms when ordering quantities of this title. For information, email info@ebooks2go.net, or call (847) 598-1150 ext. 4141. www.ebooks2go.net

Published in the United States by eBooks2go, Inc. 1827 Walden Office Square, Suite 260, Schaumburg, IL 60173

ISBN: 978-1-5457-5439-9

Library of Congress Cataloging in Publication

CONTENTS

FORWARD

We're all here for a reason. We're all here to do something great. But it's not through our job. It's through our calling. The Bible says in Ephesians 4:1 that we are to "live up to the life which God called you."

What is a calling? A worthy occupation where one derives meaning. It requires hunger and passion. It leverages the one true gift we have. Sure, we have more than one, but one stands out if you really understand yourself.

How can you understand yourself? In a relationship with God, your maker. He's who gave you your one true gift.

You see, over time, we humans have really messed things up (Genesis 3:6-24). We've made life a lot harder than it has to be. Life for us was designed to be filled with joy and happiness being in a relationship with God and each other (Genesis 2:7-25). Instead, our egos wouldn't let our will be subordinate to God's will. Consequently, our spirits got out of sync with God's spirit. Instead of spirits in harmony, they became in discord.

This book is about aligning your spirit with God's spirit, thereby enabling you to understand your true self to craft your calling. This is when you'll understand what real happiness is.

This book is not for everyone. It's written for professionals who are captives of Industrial Age thinking, systems or bureaucracy. Even though we're in the Information Age, many good people conform to antiquated business models that have not adapted to the chain-breaking freedoms that the Internet provides. Moreover, many of their *prisons* are mental prisons that require a new mindset, a new way of thinking.

This new way of thinking starts with your mind (Romans 12:2). That's the good news. You're in control.

But it's also the bad news. *Why?* Because we become what we think about and if you're dialed in to pop culture and modern "social media", then you face a real uphill battle. And the hill is very steep.

Which is why this book is not for everyone. It will take hard work and time. Patience and perseverance are required. But if you commit, then you also won't have to start your adventure alone. You'll have help.

Help from me, but also a pack of people at MindWolves who are on the same journey. Everyone is at a different point in their journey, but we're all on the same quest and willing to help. I'll be your guide, and you'll be part of a supportive community, which I call our pack.

Yes, the journey will take time, energy, and commitment. But, it will be rewarding. It will be fun. It will be worth it.

Let's get started.

DAY 1

EVERYBODY HAS A STORY

I'm sure you've heard the statement, "Everybody has a story." But have you ever really reflected on it? My guess is that it's usually used in a superficial way during *small talk* between two or more people. But it has so much meaning behind it, and in fact, truly understanding it denotes one's ability to empathize with someone else's story.

Here's a fair question to ask yourself, "Is my story working for me?" If not, then perhaps it's time to write a new story.

If your current story, which has been built over time as a function of your circumstances, experiences, and relationships, isn't taking you where you want to go, then what good is it? It's time to create the circumstances you want to craft the story you want. It's time to make lemonade out of lemons.

You don't need a new city, a new job, a new house or a new thing, but a new story. One that's different. One that's useful. One that's about opportunity and possibility. One that's about connection and trust. A story that's about your "why", "for what" and "with whom". A story that's in harmony with who you want to be. When I realized this, it changed my life for the better.

My Story

Life is messy. It took me 43 years to understand what that really means. Until then, I had experienced only two major losses in my life that triggered grief, the loss of my maternal grandmother, and my dog. As pain associated with losing a loved one goes, one might say that's pretty good. In early 2013, little did I know what was in store for me. I was about to be hurt by the person I loved more than any other in this world and in a magnitude I would not have thought was humanly possible.

I was naive. My life experiences to that point did not prepare me for what I was about to experience. I was blindsided. I was unprepared. "What is the worst thing I could do to you?" my wife asked. And then I answered the question. In hindsight, I wish I would have given a different answer. However, had I answered differently I would not have been *refined in the fire*, which has been a blessing, albeit a painful blessing.

My wife and I met in 9ᵗʰ grade. We were 14 years old. Later in high school, we were the classic *sweetheart* couple. I played football and a few other sports. She was a cheerleader. We went to the same college and somehow found a way to stay together. She never finished, but went on to have a successful modeling career in New York City. I finished my BS and MS in engineering and then took a job to be close to her. We were engaged in 1992 and married in 1994.

I have moments where I ask a lot of questions. Why her? Was I obsessed with her because she was my first love? I used to think this was a big reason, but I know now it's not. Was it because I am so physically attracted to her? Absolutely. It was as true 30 years ago as it is today. If I were to design a woman for me, with every feature thoughtfully engineered to resonate with my hormones, then she would be the result. She has an innate attractiveness that I find irresistible.

And what about her personality? While on the surface she appears to not be my type because we're so different, I have always been attracted to it. She's not boring, and I don't want boring. Perhaps deep down I knew she was what I needed. She has brought out dormant qualities in me that have made me a better person. She would say the same of me.

While my attraction to her physical beauty and personality provides some clues to the "why her" answer, it certainly does not provide the complete answer. There has to be more to explain why we are together. Our paths crossed 30 years ago and since, we've been on the same path, the same journey.

She has a dark side; in fact, she has always had it. I've never been able to completely understand it because I believe she wanted to protect me from it. In 2013, that all changed.

To simply say she had an affair is an understatement. It was premeditated. She wanted to really hurt me. She calculated with whom she would have it, a willing accomplice who would serve as the perfect terrorist for me. It was documented with more pictures than I can comprehend. I suspect there are more than her and I have accumulated in

30 years. She also constructed an alternate life on Facebook with him. It was the worst thing she could do to me, and she executed it to perfection.

Today, I suffer from post-traumatic stress disorder (PTSD), which is under control thanks to many techniques described in this book. I also suffer from depression, for which I take 20 mg of Escitalopram daily.

I share my story because by being vulnerable, I hope to become more human to you. What this book presents is not "ivory tower" thinking or some academic exercise. It's based on my real-life experiences and the need for relief from the pain. Rather than wallow in self-pity and depression, harbor hatred and the need for revenge, or seek relief by using drugs and alcohol, I decided to build my relationship with God. It is in that effort that something miraculous happened. It was not easy, but very worthwhile. It was so worthwhile that I can honestly express gratitude for the pain because, without it, I would not have found true happiness. I would not have crafted my calling. I would not be living my life to the fullest and doing work that really matters. My favorite verse in the Bible is Romans 8:28, "*We know that in all things God works for the good with those who love him, those whom he has called according to his purpose.*"

In all things give thanks, not *for all things*. Bad things happen because humans hurt other humans. We hurt each other. However, for those of us who have a genuine relationship with God, we are assured he will make a good result from the bad. It's a promise, provided you love him and submit to his will. This book is my testimony to Romans 8:28.

DAY 2

WHO'S IN YOUR BOAT?

When someone else's decision turns your life upside down, can you proceed with a calmness about you?

When someone else's mistake puts you in a difficult situation, do you gracefully handle the situation?

When you feel like you're losing everything, are you able to optimistically believe that good will result from the bad?

You are uniquely you, and you are comprised of body and spirit. Your spirit determines what your body does. It's your navigator.

On their own, our spirits are unreliable. They have a tendency to think of themselves first, others second. They are selfish in nature.

Because of this fact, our Creator gives us access to a helper, a spirit that can intercede for our spirits to help us make good decisions. The condition is that our spirits must want help. Have you ever tried to help someone who does not want help? It's impossible.

Let's call this spirit the Holy Spirit. If we allow our spirits to be subordinate to the Holy Spirit, then the answer to each of those above questions will be "yes".

It's really that simple.

Our personal lives and professional lives were never meant to be separate. They evolved that way largely because of the Industrial Age. Fortunately, the Information Age is giving us a chance to reclaim the original intent.

Therefore, let's presume your calling is the single thread that weaves everything together. It's the one thing you apply many different ways to many different situations, i.e. your role as father or mother, your job, your role as a friend, son or daughter, etc … It's what you're good at, what you like doing moment to moment, day after day, year after year. When you do it, you don't even realize you're working. Work doesn't feel like work.

When your spirit is subordinate to the Holy Spirit, and you allow yourself to be under His leadership and accept His help, then you will get to know what your calling is. The process of cultivating your calling is quite remarkable and fun. The journey itself is not easy, but the concept is simple.

Please permit me to illustrate the concept with two stories. Let's say you make your livelihood catching fish. If fact, many stories in the Bible involve fishermen. Their lives and their work were interwoven.

Story #1: Jesus and his disciples were on a boat out at sea and a storm hit. The disciples became terrified as Jesus slept like a rock. They woke him up out of fear for their lives and upon waking, Jesus calmly assured them not to be afraid and then proceeded to quiet the wind and the waves.

Story #2: After fishing for 11 hours and coming up empty, a few disciples returned to Jesus tired and depressed. He told them to immediately go back out to deep waters and cast down their nets. He also offered to join them. While skeptic, they listened to him and proceeded to catch an abundance of fish. It was the same lake, same boat, same nets, same fishermen and fish. The difference was Jesus' presence in the boat. It was a game-changer.

Now, Jesus modeled the concept of Holy Spirit subordination. He allowed himself to be under its leadership and accepted its help. He showed us how to do it. We only need to study his character, his habits, how he treated people, how he handled day to day situations. He's the ultimate player-coach. We have the benefit of knowing how he felt about things and can follow his guidance.

In both stories above, the disciples had Jesus in their boat. And because his spirit was in harmony with the Holy Spirit, it too was in their boat. In these stories, the boat is synonymous with our life's work. When we have the Holy Spirit in our boat, our life and our work is blessed with an abundance that otherwise appears out of reach. It's what guides us to build our craft.

It begs the question, "Who's in your boat?"

DAY 3

THE THREE LAWS OF HAPPINESS

Happiness is not something you find, rather it's something you create. We often look for happiness in the wrong places for the wrong reasons. We don't understand what true happiness is. True happiness is better described as joy.

There are three laws of happiness:

1. **Happiness starts in your mind.** We become what we think about, so happiness flows from right thinking. It's not a goal, but the result of cultivating a proper mindset and attitude. The word of God is for the heart of man and the way to the heart is through the mind. This is true of anything.

2. **Happiness is a choice.** If you look for happiness, you'll never find it. You're as happy as you choose to be. Happiness is not a function of your circumstances. Happiness based on feelings is fleeting, but happiness built on habits is enduring.

3. **Happiness is created from good habits.** You form habits and then your habits shape you. Habits of any kind take time to develop. They don't happen overnight. They require constant repetition to become a habit. Therefore, your focus must be on forming good habits. They are just as easy to form as bad habits, but they're more rewarding.

Like professional athletes training for their sport, you must train for your calling by internalizing these laws. Commit to mastering the habits of happiness.

DAY 4

BROKEN HEART + SLACK + WRITING = HAPPINESS

Did you know having a broken heart is a medical reality? The Mayo Clinic says "broken heart syndrome" is a temporary heart condition that's often brought on by stressful situations, such as the death of a loved one or loss of a key relationship. People with broken heart syndrome may have sudden chest pain or think they're having a heart attack.

And yes, you can die from a broken heart. Traumatic life events such as the death of a loved one, loss of a key relationship, or even an emotional memory can cause broken heart syndrome. The syndrome occurs when a surge of stress hormones causes short-term heart muscle failure. The chemicals actually temporarily weaken the heart tissue. A severe enough failure could kill you.

This makes me wonder how many people are walking around with broken hearts. I used to be one of them. Two things helped me on my journey to happiness: slack and writing. Please permit me to explain.

The most common ways for our hearts to get broken are:

- Losing a loved one by their death
- Being rejected by someone we love or we think loves us
- Holding on to resentment of others
- Feeling disappointed because things didn't turn out as we planned

Loss, rejection, resentment, disappointment all could trigger a broken heart. For me, it was betrayal, which I internalized as the feeling of rejection.

To heal the wounds of my broken heart, I first became thoughtful about downtime. By society's standards, making time for unproductive time is taboo. Competitive environments push people to reduce slack, not increase it. The reality is that systems with slack are more resilient because the extra time is not wasted. My buffer was used to clear and calm my mind, reflect, think, and be creative. It's now become a habit, and my daily rituals for intentionally creating slack have made me more productive because I'm working smarter, not harder.

Second, I learned to write, which was no small task. Writing has never been easy for me, so I had to overcome my fear of writing and lack of confidence to write. From a young age, I had conditioned my mind to think of myself as a poor writer. It was my weakest subject in school, and I scored poorly on that portion of the SATs. I forced myself to start with a journal. After a few months, I then took a giant leap by publishing a blog. That really put me out there. I'll never forget clicking the "publish" button on my first story. I literally shut my eyes and clicked! I wrote 60 whole words. Hey, it was a start.

One of my mentors, Seth Godin, said in a recent blog, "*Writing is organized thinking on behalf of persuasion … Writing may be the skill with the highest return on investment (ROI) of all. Because writing is a symptom of thinking.*"

Well said, Seth. It's certainly produced the highest ROI for me. *More than my Bachelor of Science and Master of Science in Mechanical Engineering. More than my Master in Business Administration.*

In fact, I'd be remiss to not mention the role mentors played in my healing. I surrounded myself with like-minded people from whom I learned valuable lessons. They had gone before me on a similar journey and their wisdom was invaluable.

So to wrap this up in a bow, in response to my broken heart, I first created space to clearly think, i.e. slack, and then I learned to write while getting support from mentors. Now, I am the happiest I've ever been and doing my best work, which I call my craft.

Broken heart + Slack + Writing = Happiness

Most people think of work as something you have to do because it's what society says you need to do to conform. Wake up. Go to work. Return home. Repeat. We don't want to do it, but we have to do it. Is it any wonder work feels like work for most people? It's a grind.

Not for me. My work is my craft. It's intrinsically linked to God's purpose for my life. It's where he's leading me. It's living my life in response to his love. It's what he's called me to do because he's the one who created me and knows me.

It's what I enjoy doing moment to moment, day after day, year after year. It's the single thread that weaves together my life's tapestry.

It's pure joy, pure happiness.

DAY 5

MICAH 7

Do you ever feel this way …

Poor me! I am like a hungry man,

and all the summer fruit has been picked—

there are no grapes left to eat,

none of the early figs I love.

All of the faithful people are gone;

there is not one good person left in this country.

Everyone is waiting to kill someone;

everyone is trying to trap someone else.

With both hands, they are doing evil.

Rulers ask for money,

and judges' decisions are bought for a price.

Rich people tell what they want,

and they get it.

Even the best of them is like a thornbush;

the most honest of them is worse than a prickly plant.

That was written around 700 BC. It was written by the prophet, Micah, in the Old Testament. The more things change the more they stay the same, huh?

But, here's how Micah ends his poem …

I will look to the Lord for help.

I will wait for God to save me;

my God will hear me.

Don't laugh at me.

I have fallen, but I will get up again.

He will defend my case in court.

He will bring about what is right for me.

When you have Micah's perspective, you acknowledge how the world is, but you do not conform to the world. Life knocks you down, but you keep getting back up. Why? Because you believe God is working for the good in your life. He will make things right. He specializes in turning bad into good. He will settle the score.

"All you need to do is build a relationship with Him and be patient. Wait on him. Prayerfully wait and do not act in haste." (Exodus 14:14).

The world calls this weakness. But, it's actually strength under control. I call it wisdom.

That's the paradox of depending on God. His power works best in perceived weakness. When you subordinate your will to His, you're weak. When you are weak, then He is strong in you.

DAY 6

RECALIBRATE YOUR HEART

The older I get, the more I realize how simple life is. Everything hinges on one relationship, my relationship with God.

- Are you happy and enjoying life?
- Are you where you thought you'd be at this point?
- Do you have a clear conscience?
- Do you have relief from your pain?

Let's examine the state of your heart. Be honest with yourself. Take a minute and write down the top three things you love.

What's #1? Is it God?

One of the most confusing stories in the Bible is the story about Abraham and Isaac. What kind of God would ask a father to sacrifice his son?

Abraham was very old when Isaac was born. The strength of Abraham's affection for Isaac was so strong, that Isaac quickly became the idol of his heart. The baby represented everything sacred: the promises of God, his hopes, his dreams. As he watched Isaac grow into a young man, Abraham's heart was knit closer and closer with the life of his son until the relationship became borderline dangerous. It was then that God stepped in to save both father and son from the consequences of an unhealthy love.

Then God said, "*Take your only son, Isaac, the son you love, and go to the land of Moriah. Kill him there and offer him as a whole burnt offering on one of the mountains I will tell you about.*" *(Genesis 22:2)*

God let the suffering old man go through with it up to the point where He knew there would be no retreat. Then, He forbade him to lay a hand upon the boy. In effect, He said, "It's all right, Abraham. I never intended you actually kill Isaac. I only wanted to remove him from the temple of your heart that I might be your first love."

You see, that's the strangest secret of how simple life is. Make God first in your heart, make your relationship with him most important and then all your other relationships will follow. They will be healthy and you will have a healthy perspective and balance in life.

So how do you do that?

I used to think it meant going to church and spending all this time "doing things" for God. I thought God was noticing, and it counted towards my "credit line" with him. Now I realize God cares less about the quantity of time spent with him than he does the quality of time. He cares more about the inward investment of time with him and less about the outward acts others notice.

More time with God does not mean sacrificing time with other loved ones. In fact, quality time with God enhances the quality of time and relationships with others. Making him my first love enables me to love others more.

Recalibrate your heart. In the morning and evening every day, schedule a one-on-one meeting with God. Do a spiritual inventory. Look for anything standing between you and Him and talk with Him about it. Deal with the junk from your day. It will clear your conscience.

If you form those habits, then you'll move the dial daily to a happier, more enjoyable life. You'll get to know God a little better each day.

That's all He really wants.

DAY 7

WE BECOME WHAT WE THINK ABOUT

In 1950, Earl Nightingale was inspired by the words "we become what we think about" in Napoleon Hill's book, Think and Grow Rich, around the same time he bought an insurance agency. He provided weekly motivational speeches to the agency's sales staff. In 1956, he recorded a motivational speech to be played while he was on vacation. Nightingale's employees spread word of the speech, and demand for the recording grew so large that he and friend Lloyd Conant formed the Nightingale-Conant Corporation to manage sales.

In 1957, The Strangest Secret sold over one million copies and received the first Gold Record for the spoken word, which helped launch the fields of business motivation and audio publishing. It was later adapted into print and video forms.

Nightingale postulated the secret for success in life is whatever we plant in our subconscious mind and nourish with repetition and emotion will one day become a reality. It's been proven throughout humankind, and my own life is a testimony to its truth.

When I wanted nothing more than to become an NFL coach, I made daily incremental progress toward that goal because it's what I always thought about. However, that progress was at the expense of my relationships with people I love. What I wanted most was not aligned with what was best for them. The path I thought would fulfill my purpose and give me meaning was not the course my Father in heaven wanted me to take. I was misaligned because my delight was misplaced. The desires of my heart needed to be recalibrated.

The recalibration was painful ... very painful. But I am grateful for it because of the resulting good. The lenses through which I now see life are much clearer. My mind and resolve are stronger. My heart is aligned with my heavenly Father's heart because I delight myself in Him.

Here's what I learned:

- I stopped thinking about what I want.
- Rather, I only had to think about pursuing a relationship with Him.
- That pursuit became my chief joy, my main delight.
- I became so delighted in Him that my wants became His wants.
- He filled me with the right desires and then satisfied those desires in his perfect timing and in His perfect way. I only had to be patient.
- I trusted Him as my good shepherd to such a depth that I will joyfully follow Him wherever He leads me.

I am trusting Him to lead me to where I once was afraid to go. And by doing that, others are following me. Now I clearly see the particular race I'm supposed to run and I am running it with patience, calmness, and resolve. I have not yet reached the finish line, and I am far from perfect, but I will keep on running and struggling to get the prize.

A byproduct of delighting myself in a relationship with God is better relationships with everyone else: family, friends, colleagues, and even enemies. I can do good to them without expecting to get anything back. I can be kind to all, even the ungrateful and wicked.

At home, I am a better role model for my kids and better equipped to shape them. My foundation is stronger for them. As I delight in my relationship with God, I see them delighting in their relationship with me. They are more willing to follow me and trust I have their best interests at heart.

At work and in my local community, I want to become a leader that everyone loves to follow. I believe when the leader gets better, everyone gets better. Here are seven leadership principles I've adopted:

- Thou shall not wait for permission to make things better.
- Thou shall not be afraid to make aggressive mistakes.
- Thou shall create movement, not coast.
- Thou cares, therefore thou shall persist.

- Thou has an edge because thou cares.
- Thou shall be scrappy.
- Thou shall demonstrate grit.

We become what we think about so search for delight in developing a relationship with God. Plant it in your mind and nourish it with repetition and emotion. One day, it will become a reality and you will get the desires of your heart. Then all of your other relationships will follow.

"Do not conform to the pattern of this world, but be transformed by the renewing of your mind. Then you will be able to test and approve what God's will is - his good, pleasing, and perfect will." (Romans 12:2)

DAY 8

CRAFTING YOUR CALLING

Life is simple. We tend to make it complex. Our main purpose is to love and be loved. That's why we're here. Imagine waking up every day and focusing on that simple fact. Wouldn't life be awesome?

Well, what are you waiting for? I know, I know, let me guess. You have to go to class. You need that degree. You have to go to work. You need a promotion. The kids need to go to school. You have to make more money. You need a bigger house. You don't have enough things. You need to make more "friends" on Facebook.

Since when did life become about the pursuit of more? When did we start to believe these myths:

- Having more will bring me happiness
- Having more will make me important
- Having more will give meaning to my life

More stuff is just noise. It gets in the way of our main purpose. It creates daily, self-induced stress, which is like always waking up to a cloudy, rainy day. Have you ever noticed how you feel when you wake up to a sunny day? How would you like to wake up to a sunny day every day for the rest of your life? How would you like to be both ambitious and content?

Ambition and contentment have nothing to do with each other. Contentment isn't laziness, complacency or apathy. It's enjoying what you have right now instead of waiting for something else to happen so you can be happy. It doesn't mean you don't have goals. It simply means you're happy with what you have.

I have good news for you. Gaining this perspective is possible, and you're at the right place. The process is simple, but not quick. It will require daily progress, step by step. Some days, you'll take giant leaps. Others, baby steps. Either way, you'll be headed in the right direction, and I'll be right by your side to help.

What's the secret of living in every situation, whether it's with a full stomach or empty, with plenty or little? What's the secret to always waking up to sunny days and being able to love and be loved? You must craft your calling. That's right. You get to define it. The calling you were meant to have. You're not an object aimlessly floating in the ocean of life. Rather, you're a ship in control of your destination.

"We can choose the sounds we want to listen to; we can choose the taste we want in food, and we should choose to follow what is right. But first of all, we must define among ourselves what is good." (Job 34:3-4)

DAY 9

SIMPLE IS MORE

Because we feel dissatisfied with our lives, we constantly pursue more.

- More money
- More fame
- More "friends"
- More "likes"
- More success
- More stuff

We confuse needs with wants. We're constantly grabbing at that which will never fully satisfy. Humanity's first sin was pursuing more than was intended for us. We thought we knew better and would decide for ourselves what was enough. And we're still doing it today reaching for our own forbidden fruit:

- Getting up every morning, conforming to what society says we should do, killing ourselves at work, and depleting our physical, mental, emotional, and spiritual energy.
- Wasting our money on worldly pleasures rather than investing it in things that will generate a return.
- Using our gifts on self-indulgence rather than sharing them by serving others.
- Spending our time on frivolous things that satisfy us, but are void of meaning.

We pursue more thinking our thirst will be quenched, however, it never is. Why? The answer is in a secret. The strangest secret of life is the following:

- We become what we think about.

- What we think about is what we treasure.

- Where our treasure is, our hearts will be there also.

True understanding of that secret opens the door to true happiness, a joy that can only be felt when your in a relationship with your creator and doing work you were meant to do. Have you ever heard someone say, "She's doing God's work?" Well, that's what it feels like.

How do you get there? By getting simple. Simplicity is a discipline that can be learned. It's when you prune the dead and non-fruit bearing branches of your life, i.e. the waste that depletes your energy, time, and provision that you're blessed with. It's when you make the decision to stop pursuing more. It's when you turn bad habits into good habits.

There's a way to accomplish this. It's called The Fordriven System˙. It's when you understand where you are today and incrementally change the bad to good. It doesn't happen overnight, but through trial-and-error, and with the help of a supportive coach, it will happen in time. Only then can you live a forward-driven life, rather than one looking in the rear-view mirror. That's what fordriven means. By developing the habits of happiness, you will become fordriven to craft your calling.

In other words, new habits till the soil of your heart which opens you up to forgiveness. Forgiveness is an emotional need we all have, whether we realize it or not:

- The need to *forgive ourselves*

- The need to *forgive others*

- The need to *be forgiven*

This permits new behaviors. While it's true that beliefs influence behavior, the inverse is also true. Behavior drives beliefs. New behaviors shape new beliefs, which unlocks the door to forgiveness and empowers us to feel successful. Success, in this context, is defined as the progressive realization of a worthy ideal.

And that's when you'll believe simple is more.

The Fordriven System˙: No claim is made to the exclusive right to use "system" apart from the mark as shown.

DAY 10

BALANCING PATIENCE WITH ACTION

In one of my morning rituals, I studied Exodus 14:14, "*The Lord will fight for you; you need only to be still.*" In that verse, Moses is speaking to the Israelites on the shore of the Red Sea as the Egyptian army is approaching them.

However, one verse later, Exodus 14:15 says, "*Then the Lord said to Moses, 'Why are you crying out to me? Tell the Israelites to move on.*" After reading that, I've been trying to reconcile being still with moving on. I know there is a time to be patient and a time to act. Wisdom is understanding the difference.

In these verses, are we seeing Moses' lack of wisdom, which makes him very human? I notice many people confusing patience with doing nothing and thinking God will just do something for them.

I think God expects us to prayerfully know what to do and just do it. The only way to know what to do is to have a relationship with him, which involves making time for him and having a conversation with him. In the life of Jesus, there was both prayer and action, and the balance between the two brought them into perfect harmony.

Applying this concept to our lives and work is a delicate balance. Like Moses, it's easy for us to become like a "deer caught in the headlights", patiently praying, but never taking action. The inverse is also just as easy to fall victim to. Modern society tempts us to get as much as we want as fast as we want, i.e. my kingdom come, my will be done. The only way to find perfect balance is by forming daily, weekly and annual habits that allow you to seek it.

Divert your attention from the daily chaos by scheduling 5–15 minute *meetings* with God, as needed. Withdraw one day a week from the demands of others to clear your mind and recharge your physical, mental, emotional, and spiritual energy. Abandon annually to a place where you can be "off the grid" to advance the strategic plan for your life's work.

Forge these habits, and you'll patiently weave a thread through every aspect of your life that enables you to do God's work.

DAY 11

CREATING CONDITIONS FOR REPLACEMENT

Who buys bars of soap anymore?

As I reflect on this question, I am reminded of the time my mom taught me a valuable lesson by washing my mouth out with soap. Certainly, Baby Boomers and Gen X'ers know what I'm talking about. For Millennials, kindly let me enlighten you.

Washing out the mouth with soap was a traditional form of physical punishment, typically employed by mothers and fathers, that consisted of placing soap inside a child's mouth so that the child will taste it, inducing what most people consider an unpleasant experience. It was a common form of punishment in the United States and the United Kingdom from the late 19th century through the 1970's. It was most often used as a response to profanity, lying, biting, tobacco use, or verbal disrespect. It functioned both as a symbolic "cleansing" following the infraction, as well as acting as a deterrent due to the foul aftertaste.

So there I was, an innocent 7-year old boy playing with his Matchbox cars in the dirt in his front yard. As my red '57 Chevy rounded the corner and jumped the rock, I noticed a used cigarette butt laying at the base of the hedges between my yard and my neighbor's. No one in my family smoked, but the thought never crossed my mind as to who would have discarded it. The only thing I remember is thinking that smoking was cool and that I wanted to be cool.

So I picked up the butt, placed it between my pointy and middle finger on my right hand, and pretended to puff on the cigarette, attempting to replicate all those cool people I had seen on TV. I was so caught up in the moment I had forgotten my mom had a clear line of sight from the kitchen window. I also forgot she was washing dishes and keeping an eye on me as I played with my Matchbox.

The next thing I remember was being snatched by my hair, her screaming, *"Marc David, how dare you put that filthy cigarette in your mouth? You want to smoke? I'll teach you what happens when you smoke!"*

Back then, my mom's preferred soap was Dial, and we always had a bar on the bathroom sink. Needless to say, I can still taste that Dial in my mouth. Lesson learned.

What I realize now about my mom that I did not appreciate then, is that she created the conditions where I choose new actions. From that point forward, my choices were still voluntary however; I saw a new landscape and new options. I still had free will, but she created an environment where I could make better choices.

My mom "owned" being a mom, and I am grateful that she did. My mom was a leader. She taught me, *everything is permissible, but not everything is helpful.*

Leaders understand choices are voluntary. They can't make people change, but they can nurture a culture where they choose to.

We are the sum total of our habits, personally as well as organizationally. At any point in time, these habits are either working for us or against us. What worked well at one time may not be good for us today. This is why we must be honest, humble, and vulnerable to admit when it's time to change. And change is the correct word because you can never break a habit, you can only replace it.

The best leaders and cultures understand this and they systematize it. Momentum and inertia are working for the good of good habits. Not everything that happens is good, but all things work in concert for the good.

How does this happen? Undesired habits are replaced with desired habits. Habits are more than just behaviors; they are a system of steps that generate an outcome. The behavior is merely one of the steps. The other two steps are the trigger and the reward. To replace a habit, you must examine all three steps.

1. **The trigger** – you can't control this. It's something that happens external to you.

2. **The behavior** – what you do in response to the trigger. These are crucial moments because they are your current routine.

You can control this by interrupting your impulses at these moments with a predefined alternative behavior. In other words, you will replace your current behavior with the alternative behavior until it becomes your new routine.

3. **The reward** – this is the reason your brain remembers to do new behavior and repeat the routine.

As you can see, change just doesn't happen, but you can make it happen if you replace what's not working with something that does. This simple law applies to you as well as businesses, which are nothing more than living. breathing organisms who are comprised of us, imperfect humans.

Awareness of this is the first step. Wanting to change and learn new things is the next step. After that, you literally can "replace" your way to a meaningful life doing meaningful work.

Thank you, mom, for being such a wonderful mom and leader and for teaching me that my decisions have consequences and that I own the outcomes.

Pretending to smoke that cigarette butt didn't make me a bad kid. It made me a good did who did something stupid. Beating myself up was not fruitful because I could learn from that experience and use it for the betterment of my future.

Mom, you created the conditions that allowed me to "replace" my way to a meaningful life doing meaningful work.

DAY 12

LEADERSHIP AND HAPPINESS

I read a great piece on The Black Swan Group's blog, ***The Negotiation Edge***. In an article titled, *How Leadership Failure Can Look Different Than You Might Think*, Derek Gaunt concludes:

> *"Great leaders are driven by Tactical Empathy. They understand exactly where their employees are coming from and they are governed by that perspective. At the same time, they understand that they can't do everything on their own. They know that being a leader is different than being an employee – and they act accordingly.*
>
> *All too often, leaders fail because they let their ego and their authority guide their thinking when empathy and delegation should be the real drivers."*
>
> – Derek Gaunt, The Black Swan Group,
> September 23, 2019

Derek explains what he calls The Leadership Paradox:

- Many executives don't differentiate between what they do as leaders and what they did in their previous roles.

- They may have been promoted because they were great at micromanaging, but now they're expected to work through other people.

- Facing a new challenge, they become uncomfortable – to the point where they perform their subordinates' tasks for them.

- The problem with this is that it tends to breed contempt on the part of direct reports. Employees begin thinking, "Well, if everything I do is going to be second-guessed by my manager, what's the point of doing anything?"

- Employees will either leave or, worse yet, disengage, stick around, and hurt the morale of their colleagues.

Derek points out revenge is a powerful motivator. Don't be mean to someone who can hurt you by doing nothing. Being mean includes not treating employees with respect and not letting them do the job you hired them to do.

This really resonated with me. I used to be that way, and there are still are parts of me that have trouble letting go, but I'm working to become the leader Derek describes. My happiness and the happiness of my colleagues depend on it.

It gave me pause to think about what happiness really means.

I define happiness as the progressive realization of a worthy ideal. It's the feeling of knowing where you're going, being liberated from legalism, graciously living life, and getting to know God a little better each day.

- Happy people never stop discovering, never stop stretching, never stop learning, never stop growing.

- Happiness and humility are related because humble people are coachable.

- Happy people give themselves regular checkups to ensure they don't drift from who they want to be. They test themselves regularly and if they fail the test, they do something about it. They respond well to correction.

People in leadership must realize everything starts and stops with them. They must possess a sense of extreme ownership because they control their happiness as well as the happiness of their teams.

And the first person you have to lead is yourself.

DAY 13

THE EYES OF YOUR HEART

Would you like better relationships? Have a more satisfying career? Live a more purposeful life? Then go see a *Heartometrist*, a specialist that diagnoses defects in empathy in order to prescribe corrective spiritual lenses.

Most of us go to an optometrist every year or two. In elementary school, we learn it's a good habit to form if we want to see the physical world well. The truth is that all of us are also given spiritual eyes, the eyes of the heart, which allow us to see the unseen.

Seeing the unseen is the key to empathy. Empathy is the key to better relationships, a more satisfying career, a more purposeful life. It is the cornerstone of happiness.

Behind the scenes in every workday, beyond every interaction you have with another person, past every conversation is a backstory, a context providing narrative. Any given day, you are exposed to hundreds, if not thousands, of backstories. Corrective spiritual lenses will allow you to see them clearly. The eyes of your heart will never be the same. Your life will become eternally significant.

Do I have your interest in correcting your spiritual vision? If not, then you can stop reading. If so, then kindly keep going.

Two tools a Heartometrist will use to correct defects in empathy are:

1. **Labels**

   A label is when you restate what you thought you heard the other person say in a conversation. It begins with a phrase such as the following:

- "It sounds like ... you're not happy with Sally."
- "It feels like ... you're frustrated with the position you've been put into."
- "It seems like ... you're backed into a corner."

Labels require you to actually listen to the other person and what they are really saying. Don't say anything else. Just shut up and listen.

You don't have to be perfect. Practice is the key. Employ the technique in every conversation. The other person will either tell you "that's right" or they will correct you so that you can learn how they really feel.

2. **Mirrors**

   A mirror is when you repeat, in an inquisitive tone, the last three to five words the other person says. Here's an example:

   - Other person: *"You just don't communicate well, and it's really frustrating. I'm done with you. I can't do what's expected of me because you're always leaving me in the dark."*
   - You: *"Leaving you in the dark?"*

   Rather than being defensive and escalate the conversation into an argument, just shut up and listen to what they say. They will elaborate on something specific that will be enlightening. Mirrors are very effective when used in combination with labels.

These two tactical empathy techniques will help you see what's in the other person's heart by opening up your heart to them. In doing so, your relationship with them will improve over time.

Better relationships are the fundamental building block to doing better work and finding happiness in your career. Because you spend the majority of your day at work, the positive ions you create and the empathy you acquire will be carried home with you to help you build better relationships with your family.

Commit to forming a new good habit. See your Heartometrist regularly. Practice tactical empathy with your coworkers, customers, friends, and family. Employ labels and mirrors to see better with the eyes of your heart.

DAY 14

THE HUMAN BEAKER

I stumbled across Thomas Chalmers' "*The Expulsive Power of a New Affection*" recently. Two hundred years ago, Chalmers (1780–1847) wrote it to persuade practical moralists that they cannot effectively displace from the human heart its love of the world by simply withdrawing its affection from an object that is not worthy of it. Rather, they must choose another object as more worthy of its attachment, thereby exchanging an old affection for a new one.

In a separate piece about Chalmers' "*Expulsive Power*", John Piper of DesiringGod.org presents a wonderful analogy. What's the best way to get all the air out of a glass beaker?

- You could pump it out, but the vacuum created will fill back up with air when the pump stops.

- A better method is to pour water into the beaker. The water naturally displaces all the air. It occupies 100% of the beaker. You might say it holds the #1 spot.

Now, think of your heart as the beaker. What's #1 in your beaker? What holds the top spot? What do you love the most?

Of course to the world, there's more than one answer to that question. However, there's only one answer that provides true happiness in life.

That answer is God.

In the beaker analogy, the beaker is your heart. The pump method is when we try to live life by avoiding sin. We try to avoid behaviors because we know they are not good for us, but eventually, the pump stops and we fall back to our old ways, just as the air flows back into the beaker.

As the only way to permanently displace the air is with water, the only way to lose the appetite for unwanted behaviors is to pour God into our hearts. In my experience, here's what results:

- You lead from a posture of empathy.

- You're more present with others when you're in their presence.

- You develop a pathway to peace by serving others. You understand you're completely powerless to control anyone and that each person has a will to love or reject you. Nonetheless, you choose to continually humble yourself before them and possess a servant's mentality.

- You are grateful for everything that happens, even painful things because they can shape your character for the good. All sunshine and no rain make a desert. You need the rain to nourish your God-given purpose, making it bud and flourish.

- You are generous without expectation of anything in return.

- You are patient and slow to anger.

- You judge self-righteous hypocrites, but nobody else.

- You are others-centered, not self-centered.

- You forgive so that you can focus on fulfilling your life's mission.

So, stop trying to creating a vacuum by avoiding sin. Rather, allow God to fill your heart by immersing yourself in a relationship with him daily. You'll gradually lose the taste for sin and grow in God's character.

You'll love more. You'll be happy. You'll know peace, patience, kindness, goodness, gentleness, faithfulness, and self-control.

DAY 15

WHAT'S YOUR BASELINE

Would you believe me if I said the reason you have stress in your life is because of you? You've allowed it into your life. You've opened your mind and your heart to external elements that affect your emotions. They affect your state of happiness.

It's taken me a long time to learn that circumstances, trials, work, people, and anything else external to me, do not control me. They do not have the inherent ability to steal my joy. It's only when I open my heart to them that I allow stress into my life. It comes like a thief in the night that takes what is rightfully mine. I feel stressed when I allow a deadline, a negative comment, a fellow commuter, a challenging relationship to take precedence over my peace of mind.

It begs the question … what's your baseline? What's your frame of reference from which you operate day in, day out?

My baseline, my frame is God's frame. I choose to value the fruit of his spirit … Love, Joy, Peace, Patience, Kindness, Goodness, Gentleness, Faithfulness, and Self-Control … over worldly emotions, over the stress and cares of the world. As with fertile soil, your spirit will yield whatever you plant in your mind and heart. If you plant corn, you'll get corn. If you plant black nightshade, you'll get poison.

You get to control what you plant. Nobody else does.

And why is that important? Because what's in your heart reveals what you really are. In other words, the state of your heart determines your state of happiness. Therefore, it's imperative to control what you plant. As a mirror reflects your face, your life reflects your heart.

We all have unique DNA which gives us unique fingerprints, eyes, hair, skin, voice, etc. It also gives us a unique heartbeat. Each of our hearts beat in slightly different patterns. Similarly, God has given us a unique emotional heartbeat that races when we think about the subjects, activities, or circumstances that interest us. There are certain things you feel passionate about and others you couldn't care less about. In fact, another word for heart is passion. Stress is noise that distracts us from our passion.

When you truly understand this, you will stop letting self-induced stress interfere with your life's mission, the one God gave you when he created you.

- Get control of your baseline
- Get control of your mind
- Get control of your heart

Filter out stress, focus on your passion, and pursue your mission. It's what you're called to do.

Your calling is far more significant than any job. Don't confuse it with your career. Maybe you're called to be a teacher, but that doesn't necessarily mean you'll be in a classroom. Maybe you're called to be a writer, but that doesn't mean you'll write books or work in journalism. Maybe you're called to be a preacher, but that doesn't mean you'll speak to hundreds of people every Sunday from a pulpit.

Here's something you need to believe. You have been called to become something significant. More accurately, you've been called to become like someone significant.

God knew his people in advance, and he chose them to become like his Son, so that his Son would be the firstborn among many brothers and sisters. (Romans 8:29)

It all starts with your baseline.

DAY 16

YOUR WORK: ROOT OR FRUIT?

What does the word "work" mean to you?

- Is it your job? Is it your career?

- Does it make you happy? Does it make you cringe?

- Is it something you have to do or want to do?

- Is it the root of your status and identity, or is it the fruit of your character and talents?

Here's something I've learned in my life's journey so far ...

When my greatest sense of acceptance, my wealth, my meaning, and my values are a product of my work, then I will never have enough, my relationships will be chaotic and empty and I will feel unfulfilled. On the surface, I may look like I have the perfect life, the perfect family, and have my act together, but deep down, I'm depressed and unhappy.

Fortunately, life's a two-sided coin, and I like the other side much better. I've learned my identity, my purpose, my talents are a gift from God. I don't have to earn them. I only have to graciously accept them. Then, the work I do becomes the fruit of this acceptance. My work is the reward of understanding who I am. Developing my character becomes the focus.

In other words, *who I am* is not a function of *what I do for a living*. Rather, *what I do and where I do it* is a result of *who I am*. Developing my character enables and empowers me to do everything with intention.

My happiness is not a function of my circumstances. I create the circumstances I want because I know where I'm going, I graciously live life and I get to know God, and myself, a little better each day.

DAY 17

CONTINUOUS SELF-IMPROVEMENT

Great people, great teams, great organizations have something in common. They're always getting better. They're not perfect by any stretch and make their share of mistakes, but they learn from them and move on.

When I reflect on my own life, I notice I've developed habits that nurture a continuous improvement of self. These habits serve to develop my inward being rather than obsess with the external, i.e goals, awards, promotions, possessions, and other material things. My mind, heart, and spirit are harmoniously aligned to yield the character I want to have. Every day, I get a little more loving, happier, peaceful, patient, kind, gentle, faithful, and in control of my emotions and behavior. Like David in the Old Testament, I strive to become a man after God's own heart.

This is hard work. It requires discipline, focus, and forgiveness. If I let the "daily grind" pull me through life, my circumstances dictate my happiness, I get stuck and I'm unable to make progress. I have to be intentional with my time. Accepting that I'll make mistakes and knowing that people will hurt me, I must have an eye towards learning, letting go, and pressing on.

How I spend my time empowers me to do this:

- It's alone time. No schedule, no other people, no noise, no demands. Just me and God, and I experience His presence.

- It's behind the scenes time. It's private, out of the public eye. No one sees me, except for God. I don't do it for anyone's approval, but His.

- It's not a glamorous time. It's not exciting, charmingly attractive, magical, or full of adventure. The spotlight is not on me.

I've taken to heart what the legendary John Wooden once said,

"The true test of a man's character is what he does when no one is watching ... Be more concerned with your character than your reputation, because your character is what you really are, while your reputation is merely what others think you are."

– John Wooden

DAY 18

CONTENTED AMBITION

Definitions:

Content [kon-tent] *adjective* – in a perpetual state of peaceful happiness.

Ambition [am-bish-uhn] *noun* – a strong desire to do or to achieve something significant, typically requiring determination and hard work.

Reflect on the two words above and attempt to reconcile being grateful for what you have and wanting more in life. There is a dichotomy that exists between the two desires that are challenging to bridge. Many of us living "the American dream" struggle with this reconciliation. The answer lies in our motivation.

Being grateful does not mean being comfortable. Meaningful work here on earth is never really finished, therefore we must press on, continually striving to have a greater relational impact on others. That is, after all, the only significant thing we leave behind when we die.

I am contented and can honestly say I live in a state of peaceful happiness. For that, I am grateful. However, I can also say that I am determined to continually improve my relational competency so that I can impact more lives for the better. To reach more minds and hearts to propel them into a meaningful existence. To work in service to others so that they can ascend to their highest level as a human. That's my motivation. That's what drives me.

Ambition that serves others is properly placed ambition. It does not serve one's ego or status but seeks to elevate others' acceptance of themselves, helping them feel worthy to stretch themselves to live a life of significance.

Life is not a zero-sum game when agape love is at the motivational center. Agape love is a renewable resource. The more it is given, the more there is to give. It is the highest form of love, unconditionally transcending and persisting regardless of circumstance.

It does not mean you live life wearing rose-colored glasses. It means you trust God is always working, so you can expect things to work out just as he intends them to. It enables both gratitude and ambition, i.e. the contented desire to want more of his love so that you can give more away to others.

I've spent most of my life trying to figure out what I liked, what I felt like doing, what I'm passionate about. I've taken all the personality tests, Myers-Briggs, DISC, etc ..., and many other gifts and strength tests to understand myself better. Yet, while God has designed and equipped me for a unique purpose, I believe He is asking the same question of you and me that He did of Peter in John 21:15:

When they had finished breakfast, Jesus said to Simon Peter, "*Simon, son of John, do you love me more than these?*" He said to him, "*Yes, Lord; you know that I love you.*"

Notice what Jesus did not ask Peter. He didn't ask him, "*What would you like to do with yourself when I'm gone?*" He didn't ask, "*What are you passionate about?*" Or didn't say, "*Just follow your heart.*"

Jesus simply asked if he loved him. If you can humbly answer that question in the affirmative, then you can learn contended ambition for it is born out of devotion to God above what we want or feel equipped to do.

DAY 19

LIVE GENEROUSLY

I have an amazing 12-year old daughter. She is the most generous person I know. It comes naturally to her. She doesn't give based on reason. In fact, many of her acts of kindness are illogical to her peers and many adults, myself included sometimes. Here are two recent examples:

- On a recent visit to her Pap C and Sittu (Syrian for grandmother), she received $50 cash to buy something for herself. It was one of those gifts that grandparents love to give their grandchildren *just because*. It was the only money she had in her name at that moment. The next morning, I noticed her wrapping a box for someone for Christmas.

  I asked her, "*Who's that for?*"

  She answered, "*Dallas.*" (her brother)

  "*What is it?*" I replied.

  "*The $50 Sittu gave me,*" she said.

- Her group of friends at school decided to do a Christmas gift exchange. There was an even number so everyone had someone to buy for. Names went in a hat and each picked a name. I took Jarah shopping last Saturday to take care of the friend she picked. On Tuesday, she came home from school and told me Sally decided to drop out of the gift exchange, which meant Susie wouldn't get a gift. She asked if she could buy for Susie too, which we did. I was so touched by her compassion for Susie and the forgiveness of Sally.

Jarah's generous heart is a reminder that we need to live generously. It's the right way to live, and we should never tire of it.

Our giving can reveal how happy our heart is. In fact, giving also increases our happiness. Life is not about the accumulation of things. He who dies with the most toys still dies. Life is about learning how to love. When choosing between things or people, people matter most. Use things and love people. Don't get it backwards.

One of the universal laws of nature is that we harvest whatever we plant. It's the way God wired it. In other words, we get back what we give out. In fact, we're always going to get back more than we give. This is true in every area of life, the good and the bad:

- If you give praise, praise will come back to you.
- If you give love, love will come back to you.
- If you give out gossip, people will gossip about you.
- If you get angry with others, people will get angry with you.
- If you are generous with others, other people will be generous with you.

Life is not a zero-sum game. You cannot enrich yourself by diluting others. Give of yourself without expectation of anything in return and see it returned to you with infinite abundance. It has to because that's God's law. I am so grateful Jarah intuitively understands giving what you have without regard for what you need is the proper way to live. She is a blessing to me and many others.

DAY 20

WORKING WHILE YOU WAIT

How long is too long to wait for something? When you think about it, stress is caused by our inability to wait. Stress does not get thrown onto us. In effect, we choose stress by being impatient.

Write the following life stressors on a piece of paper and then mark the level of stress you feel right now for each: high, moderate, or low.

- Finances

- Work

- Commute

- Marriage or primary relationship

- Time management

- Health, diet, and exercise

Reflecting on your answers, do you notice an inverse relationship between your patience and stress level? The less patient you are, the more stress you probably feel.

Heck, when I read the definition of patience, I naturally feel less stressed. Patience is quiet, steady perseverance; even-tempered care; diligence. To work towards something with patience is to work calmly, confidently, consistently, behaving as though it will happen. It's when you steadily, progressively persist with faith that you will accomplish your goal without concern about timing. Happily working while you wait is key to less stress.

For any good and worthwhile thing, there is an ideal time to receive it. Timing is crucial. Many times, it may be the right thing, but the wrong time. In every area of your life, there is perfect timing. Your education, your job, your marriage, your family, your retirement all have perfect times. That timing is called God's timing. When you get in front of, or behind, God you induce stress on yourself.

Spiritually maturity is the ability to wait. Faith is waiting for the answer. When you don't get what you want when you want it, God isn't necessarily saying "no". He may only be saying "not now".

Just keep mindfully working, and listening, while you wait. Eventually, the perfect time will manifest itself, and it will be worth the wait.

DAY 21

SAVOR TODAY

With an unreconciled past and uncertain future, we have a tendency to be unappreciative in the present. A common result of such ingratitude is conformance with what we think society wants us to do, which grinds us into something we don't like. That's no way to live.

Such are the difficult, routine, and monotonous tasks of daily work and life, a.k.a. the daily grind. It's a byproduct of Industrial Age culture, which still exists in corporate America and many other parts of the world. The grind effectively constructs personal prisons that entrap our spirits. It does not serve us well and prevents us from savoring the beauty of today.

Learning to savor today frees all those who are held in that prison. Yes, the good news is that you can learn how to escape. Think of it as training, much like an athlete trains for their sport. It's not easy, but is simply accomplished by pursuing these four steps with an indomitable spirit:

1. **Know** your God-given identity.

    • It's is only possible by developing a relationship with God.

    • It helps you understand what's expected of you (and what's not). This is your calling.

2. **Accept** the responsibility for your calling.

3. **Change** your priorities.

    • Redefine your values and what's important.

    • Reassign your priorities.

    • Trim the vine of anything that is not aligned with those priorities.

4. **Look** ahead to the goal in faith.

    •   Keep your eye on the reward.

    •   Faith means being sure of the things we hope for and knowing that something is real even if we do not see it.

Faith is also remembering great people who lived in the past and who demonstrated, with perseverance and grit, that executing these four steps is possible. I can think of people from biblical times through the present day who've accomplished this. I am grateful to have them as role models.

One such person is Moses. When he eventually learned his true identity, i.e. he was a Jew and not the grandson of the King of Egypt, he chose to accept responsibility for freeing the Hebrews from slavery from Pharaoh. He gave up all the things many people spend their whole lives trying to get: popularity, pleasure, and possessions. He rejected the luxurious life. This newfound responsibility set his vision, his vision influenced his values, and his values determined his priorities. He ultimately leads the Hebrew people out of slavery, but it was a long and arduous journey. It took an enormous amount of grit and faith by keeping his eye on the reward.

Moses was able to savor every day of that journey because it was rooted in a daily relationship with God. That's the common denominator for our journeys as well. He let go of his past, faithfully walked to his future, and embraced his present. The same opportunity is available to us.

Know. Accept. Change. Look. Four simple steps.

God longs to do far more than you ask or think, provided you lean into him for his guidance. He has plans for you far above anything you could ever dream, and the path to those plans begins by savoring today.

DAY 22

TRAIN FOR YOUR CALLING

<u>Definitions:</u>

Calling [kaw-ling] *noun* – a worthy occupation where one derives meaning; requires hunger and passion

Train [treyn] v*erb (used with object)* – to be taught through practice and instruction; requires humility and coachability

Success [suhk-ses] *noun* – the progressive realization of a worthy ideal; requires persistence and grit

Aren't we all in search of life's Holy Grail, i.e. that elusive thing with miraculous powers that provides happiness, wholeness, and sustenance in infinite abundance, that thing which helps us feel significant? Without it, we feel inadequate and incomplete, and we're just going through the motions.

Many people incorrectly think their calling is something that is found. They wander through life with a hunger to find meaning in their work, yet struggle to do work that matters. How many worthwhile things in life are found versus created? An extreme sense of ownership is needed to create your calling. It's not accidental. Rather, it must be intentional. You must train to receive your God-given gifts.

As long as your motivation is right, whatever you do can become a calling. That means menial tasks become meaningful tasks when they do them out of love for God and others. When you view what you do as serving humankind, everything you do becomes significant.

If you would have told me 30 years ago I would cultivate my calling by selling insurance, I would have laughed and laughed and laughed. As a mechanical engineer graduating from a top engineering program, my ego ensured I looked down upon the sales profession and insurance industry. I was too educated for that type of job.

When I reflect on my motivational tipping point, the root cause holding me back was my ego. I was too proud, and the only thing that did was guarantee my unhappiness. It was humility that unlocked true happiness and enabled me to create my calling. I had to learn how to be humble, and I accomplished this by training my mind and heart to serve others.

I was, and still am, tested in this all the time. For example,

- When I walk outside of my office and see trash on the ground, do I pick it up or let someone else do it?

- When I walk outside the grocery store and put my bags in my car, do I take the cart back or let someone else do it?

- Do I do the household chores I despise as a way to serve my family, or do I let my kids do them?

The humble choice isn't always an easy one, but the humble choice to serve others rather than expecting others to serve you will transform your relationships and lead to lasting happiness.

It was only by becoming humble that I discovered I was already perfectly and completely loved, liked, and enjoyed by God. I learned humility was a prerequisite to have a genuine relationship with Him. Only then was my motivation right, and I was finally free to train for my calling and view myself as a success.

Society defines success as the attainment of wealth, status, honors, or the like. That could not be further from the truth. Training for your calling entails re-calibrating your mind to define success as the progressive realization of a worthy ideal. As long as you're making progress toward your calling, then you're a successful person.

Your calling is like an infinite football field, and you're the feature running back. Focus on *moving the chains.* You have four plays to get the first down. Many plays will result in positive yardage. Some will be for a loss. Others no gain. On average, net 10 yards every 4 plays, and you'll progressively move the chains down the field.

DAY 23

A RHYTHM TO LIFE

There's a rhythm to life, a strong, regular, repeated pattern of doing the right thing at the right time. Every minute of every day, we are either in or out of rhythm. I gained a true appreciation for this a few days ago as I rang in the new year.

<u>Testimony #1</u>

In October, I received a $250 gift card for Eddie V's, an upscale seafood restaurant in Pittsburgh. It's not the typical restaurant at which I would treat my kids to dinner because it's very expensive. My 15-year old son typically eats two dinners, so I estimated he'll account for $200 of the $250. My 12-year old daughter typically eats chicken fingers and fries, and I didn't see that on the menu. However, I did notice a nice crab legs appetizer I hoped she'd eat. Nonetheless, I decided to take the risk and booked a 5 pm New Year's Eve reservation at Eddie V's.

At that time, the valet was not working so I had to park my SUV in a nearby parking garage. I dropped my family off at the restaurant and proceeded to the garage. It had been a few years since I parked in this particular garage and was unaware that the maximum height was lowered to just 6 ft. I had assumed my SUV would fit from what my memory served as the old height clearance, but I was suddenly worried about the new height limit.

As I pulled the ticket, the gate opened and I slowly proceeded under the height bar. The first few inches appeared to be OK. I winced as I listened for the noise of the steel bar rubbing my roof rack. Nothing ... *whew*.

Then about half-way through, I heard the bar hit and rub the rest of the way. Shoot, I thought to myself. I'm in, but now what should I do?

I heard an attendant yell, "*Hey, what are you doing? That thing's too big for this garage.*"

I said, "*I'm sorry. It seemed like it would fit, but by the time I realized it, it was too late. I was in. What should I do?*"

At that moment, I expected him to instruct me to turn around and exit the garage without going any further.

"*I'll take care of you. Just leave it there with the keys in it,*" he answered

Wow! How nice of him, I thought. "*Thank you so much sir,*" I replied.

That act of kindness made the rest of the evening perfect. Without it, I would have had to circle the streets of Pittsburgh looking for a spot on New Year's Eve. Needless to say, it would not have been easy.

After dinner, I left my family behind at the restaurant to get my SUV and realized I only had a $20 and $50 bill in my wallet. In my mind, I was planning to tip the friendly attendant $10. That was a fair tip; given the cost to park was $6. *What to do?*

I arrived at the garage; saw my truck and the attendant. At that moment, I made a poor decision. I did not do what I should have done. I thanked him, told him how much I appreciated his help, and proceeded to exit the garage without tipping him. I felt bad, really bad. After all, I did not have $10 to give him. Rightfully so, he looked visibly disappointed and didn't say anything except, "*You're welcome.*"

I could have asked if he had change for a $20, but that didn't seem right. I could have said I needed to get change and will be back, but thought that would only elicit a "Yeah, right." Instead, I drove off saying nothing but thinking I'll get change for my $20.

As I circled back to pick up my family on Pittsburgh's busy Grant Street, getting change wasn't in the cards. *Boy, did I botch this up,* I said to myself. At that time, I finally made the right decision.

I drove back to the garage, turned on my SUV's flashing hazard warning lights, and looked for the friendly attendant. We made eye contact.

He asked, "*Where did you come from?*"

I replied, "*I wanted to give this to you. Happy New Year. Thank you for being so nice to me.*"

I handed him the $20. He was so surprised. "*Thank you, man. I appreciate it. Happy New Year.*"

Testimony #2

The next morning on New Year's Day, I had to run out to get gas. I pulled up to the pump at my local GetGo, got out of my SUV, loosened my fuel cap, and heard someone say, *"Excuse me, are you a local?"*

I looked up to see who was talking and suspiciously answered, *"Yes, I live around here."*

"The Lord told me to approach you. I'm driving from North Dakota to Philadelphia. I was wondering if you would help me?" he asked.

"What did you have in mind? What kind of help do you need?," I asked.

"I'm recently divorced and on my way to a new life. I have a job lined up in Philly. I need gas to get there and a little food. I'm a carpenter and have a job waiting for me. I just need a little help.," he answered.

There was something about this guy. He was genuine, credible. I looked at his car. It had North Dakota plates. It also looked like it had been on the road for a while and through all sorts of weather.

I normally don't have cash on me, but I still had the $50 bill in my wallet from the night before. I said to him, *"I'll believe that you're telling me the truth. I have $50 on me. Would that be enough?"*

He nodded affirmatively. I handed him the $50.

He then asked, *"Are you a SEAL?"* (I was wearing my SEAL Team hat).

"Actually, no, but my brother-in-law is in the Navy, and I love the SEALs.," I humbly replied.

"I think they tell you guys not to tell anyone you are," he replied smiling and grateful.

That was the last thing he said to me as I proceeded to fill up my tank and watch him top off his tank and buy a little food.

Walking in the Spirit

These two experiences touched my heart. They taught me there is a rhythm to life. Learning to do the right thing at the right time takes skill. People who believe in God, as I do, label that skill "walking in the Spirit." The deeper your relationship with God grows, the better you get at that skill. Sometimes God's Spirit leads you to run fast. Other times, He leads you to walk slowly. Knowing when to act fast and when to act patiently is part of mastering the skill. Both scenarios require balancing action and discernment.

This year, God will put people in your life with needs. Some may be physical needs. Others emotional, mental, or spiritual. Don't withhold good from those who deserve it when it's in your power to help them. If you wait for perfect conditions, you will never get anything done.

There's never a perfect time to do anything. All of us must quickly carry out the tasks assigned to us by God, for there is little time left before our work comes to an end.

DAY 24

THE PROBLEM OF WHY

In his book, *The Problem of Pain*, C.S. Lewis says that pain plays an important role in the development of human character. Pain may lead someone to repent, but it also may lead them to bitterness. Hell exists for those who won't repent no matter how great the pain. Simply stated, in hell, God makes room for those who are not interested in Him.

Which leads to The Problem of Why.

In my own life, I was least interested in God when I asked "why?" the most. I kept asking why and wasn't getting any good answers:

- Why did this happen to me?
- Why did "so-and-so" hurt me?
- Why can't I do this?
- Why can't I have that?

Any expert on problem resolution knows the "5 Whys" technique. You can get to the root cause of any problem by asking why up to five times. The technique doesn't work with worldly pain.

The other morning, I had a conversation with my 12-year old daughter on her way out the door to school. It was 19°F, yet she was wearing a short-sleeve shirt and no jacket.

I said to her, *"You need a jacket. It's only 19° outside."*

"Why?" she asked.

"Because it's too cold to only wear short-sleeves," I answered stating the obvious (to me).

"Why?" she asked again.

"Because it's also going to snow today," I added.

"Daaaaad, why? I'm only going to be outside for a few minutes. From the car to the bus, from the bus to the school," she argued.

"Jarah, just put on a jacket. Sometimes, it doesn't matter why. Just do what I say," I said sternly.

That conversation reminded me of many I had with God in the past. Until I stopped asking why I wanted answers from Him about the pain and disappointment in my life. It was only when I stopped asking that I became interested in what He had to say. That's when I learned about vulnerability-based trust.

Vulnerability-based trust is the foundation of strong relationships. Whether it's a team of 2 or a team of 11, it's the key ingredient on which cohesive, high-performing teams are built. I allowed myself to be transformed when I allowed myself to be vulnerable to God. Now my spirit and His spirit are a cohesive team of 2.

Encountering God is similar to encountering another person. I don't seek an experience with that person. Rather, I seek to know him or her by spending time with them, and I gain experience as a result. I don't seek to hear their voice. I simply engage in conversation as an act of wanting to know them and hear their voice as a result. The only thing that is different about seeking God is that He is Spirit, not flesh. Spend time with His Spirit and gain experiences as a result. Engage in conversation with His Spirit and hear His voice as a result.

What does vulnerability look like during an encounter? It's acknowledging you're human and not perfect. Humble recognition of this fact opens the door to personal honesty, confession, forgiveness, and the Fruit of the Spirit in relationships (Love, Joy, Peace, Patience, Kindness, Goodness, Gentleness, Faithfulness, and Self-Control).

Vulnerability-based trust with God is the launchpad to living a life beyond mediocrity, to living an excellent life worthy of your calling. In Ephesians 4:1 we are told to "live up to the life to which God called you."

Vulnerability-based trust with people is the stuff great teams are made of. Learn it. Live it.

Stop asking why. Forgive yourself. Forgive others. Let go of the past and your pain. Drive forward with a vulnerability-based trust in God and your teammates.

DAY 25

TEAM C

I've had the same license plate since 1998, TEAM C. Back then, I wanted COACH C, but it was unavailable in the Commonwealth of Pennsylvania. I "settled" for TEAM C, and little did I know how prophetic it was. Twenty-two years later, TEAM C embodies my calling.

Life has a specific design, a way in which it is intended to work. It's meant to be lived in community with others, in other words as a team. One can only live a meaningful life in the context of a team. Everyone's team is different, yet we all have the same purpose, to use our Spirit-empowered gifts and resources to build up the whole team to accomplish our God-given mission on Earth. Investing in the lives of your teammates serves them and the greater good of the team. Our individual motive should be to sacrifice ourselves so that our teammates can do even greater things than us.

Most people act as if living a meaningful life is all about status, having the lofty title, living in the exclusive neighborhood, making a lot of money, driving the fanciest car. In team speak; this is equivalent to having all the right *statistics*. It's like having a team comprised of star players who are individually successful, however that does not guarantee a cohesive, successful team. In fact, my experiential belief runs counter to that prevailing wisdom.

I believe meaning and purpose are derived by our individual contribution to a team that has players willing to sacrifice personal success for the sake of the team. Players who forget about their own statistics to get the win. Players who subordinate their ego for the benefit of the team.

Back when I wanted COACH C on my license plate, I had an individualistic motive. I wanted Coach C, the nickname given to me my players because my last name was hard to pronounce, to get the glory. I wanted Coach C to get the praise. Sure, I wanted the team to win, but so I could get the accolades.

By settling for TEAM C, I did not realize then that God was giving me an aiming point. I had a hunger to be a coach and teacher, but I had the arena all wrong. Rather than football, my "sport" was to be a professional workplace. Rather than football players, my "athletes" were to be faith-led people who were entrapped by the 9–5 daily grind and trying to live the "American dream." TEAM C was to be my beacon as I chart my life's course. Having the benefit of hindsight and a little wisdom, I see that now.

TEAM C helps me to navigate through the good days and bad days. On good days, it keeps me humble and reminds me that I'm part of something bigger than myself. On bad days, it keeps me focused on my mission and helps me weather the storms. Every day, it points me to my purpose, which is to train professionals for their calling. I'm called to serve and invest in them so that they can do even greater things than me, and we all serve a God who gets all the glory.

DAY 26

ADVERSITY, THE GREAT TEAM BUILDER

Today, I'm writing on location at The SPIRE Center, a multi-sport complex in Geneva, OH. My daughter has taken up club volleyball and this is her first of many tournaments. I enjoy the change of pace from my normal morning routine. I'm also grateful for the beautiful fresh dusting of snow on the ground. There's nothing like a layer of God's fresh white powder to transform an otherwise mundane landscape into a beautiful work of art. I appreciate God's purpose for snow, to slow us down, in the midst of our busy schedules and regular tasks, so we can simply rest in his good gifts.

My daughter's team is designated a 12-year old team, however, they have only two 12-year old girls. The majority are 10 and 11, and they are the youngest, most inexperienced team here. The teams they're up against are older, bigger, stronger, and have been playing together for a couple of years. Their first match revealed that disparity.

Needless to say, yesterday morning was a long morning. They lost every set of every match. Their confidence was low and their coaches did their best to teach them and pick up their spirits. After a long mid-day break, they got back at it.

The afternoon was much better. They won their first set after the break and took their opponent into the third set of a best of three matches. They ultimately lost the last set, but they fought valiantly. They started to function as a team and exhibited moments of perfection. Dig, set, kill. Their confidence and cohesion rose as they competed throughout the afternoon. There were blood, sweat, and tears. They fought the good fight, and the simultaneous look of exhaustion and satisfaction on their faces revealed it. The "well done" they received from their coach was a great way to cap the day.

The adversity they faced was a reminder of what a great team builder it can be, provided the response to it. Everybody has a role. Everyone has a job to do. One person not doing their job means the whole team is off. The coach has to remind the players of that, using bad decisions and unforced errors as constructive learning tools. No one person is above the team. Nobody can do it all themselves. They have to use and trust their teammates. There can't be one hero getting all the glory, but rather everyone must unselfishly serve their teammates and make heroes of them.

Life is a team sport, and the common good is served by viewing it that way. God will use anyone who believes in him to change the world for the better. Each of us must continually ask, "Am I trying to be the hero, or am I trying to make heroes of others?" All adversity works for the good for those who love him and are called according to his purpose.

There should be no division of *the team* if its members have equal concern for each other. If one member suffers, every member suffers with them. If one member is honored, everyone celebrates with them. The team grows and builds itself up in love, as each member does their job. Just as every person has one body with multiple parts with different functions working together, a team is comprised of many members with different talents and roles. The team forms one body and each member belongs to all the others.

To the 2020 Revolution 12U team, thank you for the reminder. You set a wonderful example of how to use adversity to build a cohesive team.

Well done.

DAY 27

BE A NEIGHBOR

The late, great Fred Rogers treated everyone like a neighbor. I think most people interpret that word literally, i.e. a person living near or next door.

Mr. Rogers, however, had a broader definition. To him, everybody is our neighbor. He humanized our world better than anybody in modern history.

"Love is at the root of everything. All learning. All relationships. ...

It's an invitation for somebody to be close to you. ...

The greatest thing we can do is to help somebody know that they're loved and capable of loving."

– Fred Rogers

I am humbled that Mr. Rogers and I share the same neighborhood, literally and figuratively. We're both from Pittsburgh, PA. I grew up watching his TV show, which was produced by WQED in Pittsburgh. He taught me two very valuable lessons:

1. Prioritize **likeness over differences**
2. Put **others over self**

Coincidentally, these are also lessons taught by Jesus in The Parable of The Good Samaritan, a story about what it looks like to be a neighbor. In that story, a question is asked, "And who is my neighbor?" (Luke 10:25-37)

Both Mr. Rogers and Jesus had the same answer. We are all human and made in the likeness of God. Rather than focus on how we're different … race, gender, political or religious beliefs … we should acknowledge we are all humans who need to know we are loved and are capable of loving others.

We should also place others above ourselves by seeing their problems as our problems. Why? Because the people in our lives are more important than our plans or agenda. We should enter the mess of their lives and make them our own.

When Mr. Rogers extended the invitation, *won't you be my neighbor?* he was genuinely humanizing each of us and modeling the behavior of a loving neighbor. It was the same model of love the Good Samaritan offered to the beaten, nearly dead stranger on the side of the road.

This standard of behavior is hard. It shouldn't be, but it is. The reason it's hard is because it's counter-cultural. Society doesn't teach unconditional love, selfless sacrifice, and self-control. Rather, it promotes selfish love and "have it your way". In fact, because we're flooded with these messages daily, the force of their current acting on our behavior is so strong that many of us get caught up in it. For most of my life, I certainly was.

But now, I am grateful for the seed that was planted in my heart as a child is starting to blossom. I am grateful for the lessons I was taught about how to be a good neighbor and who my neighbor is. I am grateful for the ability to prioritize **likeness over differences** and **others over self**. I am grateful for the willingness to enter the mess of other people's lives and make them my own. I am grateful for my calling, which is to train others on how to **be a neighbor** too.

DAY 28

GOD'S EXAMPLE

Last February my son, Dallas, wanted to work for Chick-fil-A. Being only 14 years old, he was a little young, but he gave it a shot. I helped him by picking up the application, filling it out, and coordinating the interview with the restaurant manager for him. As he interviewed, I waited in the car for him to return. He had butterflies, which is normal for a first job interview. I was probably more nervous than him. After all, what parent wants to see their child rejected?

He returned to the car, and I asked, "*Well, how'd it go?*"

He replied, "*Good, but I was told I'd be better for Back of House, and you have to be closer to 16. She told me to apply again next year around the same time.*"

As he counted the passing twelve months, his desire to work for Chick-fil-A did not wane. If he had it his way, we'd eat dinner there every night. Plus, he loves their culture and corporate values and wants to be part of their team.

This time, however, I decided not to do everything for him. Rather, I would counsel him through the process and teach him what he'll have to do to make the right impression to get the job. I want him to benefit from the knowledge of how to get the job, rather than him benefiting from the direct results of my labor. He would have to be responsible, accountable, and earn it himself.

He picked up, filled out, and turned in the application on his own. His cell phone and e-mail were listed as contacts, not mine. He would get the call to coordinate the interview.

He turned in the application late Monday evening. He received a call Wednesday to schedule the interview for <u>next</u> Friday.

I asked him, "*Is that Friday, February 14ᵗʰ or Friday, February 21ˢᵗ?*"
He replied, "*Next Friday is the 21ˢᵗ.*"
I said, "*Ok, just make sure you confirm what date she meant.*"

So, I'm relaxing from an exhausting week late on Friday the 14ᵗʰ, and Dallas pops his head into my room, "*Dad, I just listened to a voice message from Chick-fil-A. My interview was today, and I missed it.*"

"*I'm so sorry about that, Dallas. Did you confirm what 'next Friday' meant?*" I asked.

"*No, I was certain it was the 21ˢᵗ,*" he answered.

"*Well, I think you should call them back, apologize for the misunderstanding, and I'm sure they will forgive you and reschedule,*" I advised.

Dallas' interview was rescheduled for Monday, February 17ᵗʰ. It was a valuable learning experience for Dallas.

As Dallas grows up, he's becoming a more coachable young man. He's allowing me to "prune" him, just as I allow God to prune me. It's becoming more and more evident to me that Dallas notices that. My process of discipline and correction is aligned with God's process, and it's rooted in unconditional love. We treat every day as an opportunity to grow in relationship with His Spirit and allow the pruning of branches that do not bear fruit. Every gardener knows that pruning non-bearing fruit branches of a vine or a plant returns even more fruit on the fruit-bearing branches. This is analogous to how we should live our lives.

As I reflect on this Chick-fil-A experience, it highlights how important it is to learn by doing and making room for failure. We are all better off if we acquire the knowledge of how to do something rather than simply getting something itself. We can't appreciate what we don't work for.

For example, children are better off learning how to get a job and make money rather than getting the money itself. They are better off getting the example of their parents' labor rather than the result of their parents' labor.

I am grateful for the example that God sets for me so that I may set it too for others that I care about and love like God loves me.

DAY 29

THE KEY

In my experience, forgiveness is not easy, but it's the key that unlocks the door to fulfilling God's mission for ourselves on Earth. We have to commit to self-mastery of forgiveness to clearly see our purpose and mesh it with our calling.

Forgiving goes against our nature to fight back, harbor hurt, and have the last word. However, we don't have to rely solely on our own strength. If you're a believer, you can trust you have the Holy Spirit working in you to help choose the things God loves, i.e. mercy, compassion, and grace. You can show these things to those who offend or hurt you because that's what he's shown to you.

"Love prospers when a fault is forgiven, but dwelling on it separates close friends." (Proverbs 17:9)

The world right now is having an identity crisis and misunderstands what love really is. Love is not what you feel or say. It's what you do. It's an action. To forgive is to love.

With the rise of the Internet and social media, we can now project ourselves as anything we want. Many work tirelessly to build up a false self so that they can receive affirmation from others. Others use it as a platform to get even and have the last word. At the root, both camps are exposing their greatest need, i.e. to be loved. It is, in fact, humanity's greatest need, and we have an enemy aimed at its destruction. Putting on facades to our true identity is exactly what the enemy wants. It forces us into a lifestyle of never being truly known and therefore never truly loved for who we really are.

Forgiveness is the weapon that will defeat the enemy. Learning to forgive yourself and forgive others means you will let go of the past, wipe the slate clean, and start over with a "clean sheet of paper".

It's never too late to forgive. In fact, I would argue that life really doesn't start until you do. It's the key to unlocking the door to your true self and your calling.

DAY 30

ARE YOU AFRAID TO DIE?

I'm sorry. Please forgive me. I'm calmly, assertively, and peacefully living my life. I refuse to sop up the hysteria and participate in the panic. There's good news about the current state of COVID-19 that's not being promoted.

I respect the seriousness of the pandemic. It's a highly contagious virus. I pray for the health and safety of those who have compromised immune systems, as they are the most vulnerable. For the majority of the general population, I struggle to see how the risk justifies the panic.

For someone like me, the risk is suffering from flu-like symptoms, not death. Frankly, for the past 50 years, I've lived with that risk. Because COVID-19 is so easily spread, I've enhanced my personal hygiene practices and respect the need for social distancing, but other than that, my behavior is normal.

The only rational explanation of the panic is the fear of death. Even though death is an improbable outcome of catching the virus, its uncertainty is causing irrational behavior. Why? Perhaps it's a revelation of how little humans want to think and talk about death?

The current state of society is a great example of what happens when we let our fear of death paralyze us. It begs reflection about what's possible when the inverse is true when you're not afraid to die when you're not afraid to take informed, calculated risks?

When you know where you're going, you know the ending. No matter what twists and turns you take, eventually, you'll navigate to your final destination. You can proceed with calm confidence, even though storms will attempt to derail you. You will persist until you arrive. In fact, persistence is another word for faith, for when you have faith, you will persist.

I know the end to my life. I will die. I can't avoid it. However, I also know my purpose while I'm here. It's to love God first and then love others by serving them with joy, peace, patience, kindness, goodness, gentleness, and faithfulness. It's to exhibit self-control whereby I place their interests above mine. I know that I can fulfill that purpose with my calling, which is to be a professional coach. Not a coach of a professional sport, but a coach of professionals in the workplace who have to balance work with the demands of family and community. I am called to train them to gain clarity about their purpose and to help them craft their calling.

When one understands purpose and calling, then death is no longer a scary proposition. I am not afraid to die because I know where I'm going, and I have faith I will get there. I don't know when or how, but I know the ending.

Because I'm not afraid to die, I am no longer paralyzed by worldly worries. A new frontier of possibilities is opened to me. Instead of asking, *"Why is this happening?"* I'm asking, *"What's possible?"* My hope is that you can experience this too. Calm, assertive, peaceful energy is greatly needed.

Call to Action: START YOUR ADVENTURE

Since you were a child, you've dreamed about "doing what you love, what you're passionate about." You see yourself working in a utopian world where work doesn't even feel like work, you are good at it, you enjoy doing it moment to moment, day after day, year after year, and you feel successful, valued, and loved.

At this point in your life, what is your response to the following statements, "yes or no"?

- I can control the busyness of my life.
- I do not feel pressured to do what everyone else is doing.
- I am not stressed to keep up with my neighbors, friends, and family.
- My self-worth is not derived from status symbols, i.e. car, house, zip code, job title.
- I can suppress the need to get even when someone hurts me.
- I am not afraid of anything.
- I feel important.
- I don't care if people like me.
- I am not driven by my career.

If all your answers were *NO*, then you're at the right place. You found this book for a reason, and I am grateful you did.

In 2013, all my answers were *NO*. Now, they are *YES*. What changed? Me.

Now, I understand my unique ability to use for good in the world. I love the work I do. I have better relationships with others. I am a happier person. I am a generous and grateful person, no matter my circumstances. I have a calm, assertive posture in life.

I want the same for you. To start your adventure, take the free MindWolves Awareness Assessment by visiting mindwolves.com/awareness.

AFTERWARD

I know that you and I have at least one thing in common. There is a door opened to each of us for something beautiful to be worked out in our life. I saw the door and walked through it. Have you? If not, then look for my hand stretched out for you. Take it and let me show you what's possible.

On the other side of the door, we have to first discuss authority. That is, under whose authority do you do anything? If we get this answer wrong, then we may as well turn around and walk back out the door. The only way we can stay on this side of the door of opportunity is to submit to God's authority. It's ok if you don't want to. That's your choice. But if you do, then trust it will be worth it.

What does that actually mean? It simply means that if God wills, you will do. Implicit to that statement is obedience to His principles, and a hunger to understand his teachings, a willingness to be obedient to it, and humility to let your will be subordinate to His. It also means that you have an acknowledgment that it is He who enables the good that arises out of the mess of your life because in all things he is working for your good. This is the opportunity that is common to us.

On this side of the door, obedience comes from faith in his word. As a result of our faith, our desire is to be obedient to his authority.

The cool thing about being on this side of the door is that God will be working out something beautiful with your life even if the world knows almost nothing about you. The type of beauty I'm talking about is relational and meaningful. It's not based on popularity. It's counter-cultural. It's about serving others with neighborly love so that they want to follow you through that same door we all have in common.

www.ingramcontent.com/pod-product-compliance
Lightning Source LLC
Chambersburg PA
CBHW040929210326
41597CB00030B/5237